Funeral Director and Mortuary Exam Study Book

Copyright

Funeral Examining Board

Editor/Publisher Noaha

Edition 1 (1991)

New Revised Edition 5 (2023)

All rights reserved. No part of this book may be reproduced or transmitted in any form or by any means, electronic or mechanical, including photocopying, recording, or by any information storage and retrieval system, without written permission from the Publisher.

The International Conference of Funeral Service Examining Boards administers a National Board Examination (NBE) to evaluate the knowledge needed to become a licensed funeral director or embalmer.

Funeral Service Test scores are used by the International Conference of Funeral Service Examining Boards as a uniform standard of qualification. While it may not be fair, all of a person's plans for the future may be dependent upon needing a certain Funeral Service Test score.

That is the purpose of this study guide: to give test you the keys to understand how to succeed on the Funeral Service Test.

If you would like to get the Funeral Service Test score you deserve and to quit worrying about whether your score on the Funeral Service Test is good enough, then study this book thoroughly.

Many students use the wrong strategy, but you can avoid the pitfalls with the help of this book.

Last Will and Testament

When a person dies without a will, he is said to have died intestate. An intestate estate is also one where the will presented to the court has been deemed to be invalid. A last will and testament does not take effect until you're deceased, and is separate from a health care directive, sometimes referred to as a "living will," which focuses on your medical treatment while you're still alive.

A will is an instrument for the ordered disposition of real and personal property that is to take effect upon death. Which of the following is a requirement for a will to take effect?

○ The will has a codicil.

○ The deceased was of legal age.

○ There was intestacy on the part of the legatee.

○ Both B: and C:

How a Last Will and Testament Works

A will and last testament directs the disposition of your assets, such as bank balances, property, or prized possessions. It will detail who is to receive property and in what amount. It can establish guardian arrangements for surviving dependents.

A person writes a will while living. Its instructions are only carried out once the individual dies. A will names an executor of the will. That person is responsible for administering the estate. A probate court usually supervises the executor to ensure that the wishes specified in the will are carried out.

A will and last testament can form the foundation of an estate plan and is the key instrument used to ensure that the estate is settled in the manner desired by the deceased.

While many people obtain assistance with their wills from a lawyer, this is not necessary to make most wills legal and binding.

What a Will Doesn't Do

There are several situations after death for which a will isn't useful.

Disposition of Certain Property

- Property held in joint tenancy with someone else
- Property assigned to a living trust
- Life insurance policies with designated beneficiaries.
- A pension plan, individual retirement account (IRA), 401(k) plan, or other retirement plan with designated beneficiaries.
- Financial assets (such as stocks and bonds) held in accounts that already have completed beneficiary forms.
- Money in a payable-on-death bank account.

A will is an instrument for the ordered disposition of real and personal property that is to take effect upon death. Which of the following is a requirement for a will to take effect?

    a. The will has a codicil.

    b. The deceased was of legal age. `Correct`

    c. There was intestacy on the part of the legatee.

    d. Both B: and C:

The deceased was of legal age. This requirement must be met for the will to take effect after the demise of the individual. A will completed by a minor who dies while still a minor is not recognized as a legal will. A codicil is a formal addition to a will, but it is not a requirement for a will to take effect. The legatee is the person who is to inherit the personal property specified in the will. Intestacy is the condition that occurs when a person dies and has no will.

The FTC's Funeral Rule

It enforced by the Federal Trade Commission (FTC), makes it possible for you to choose only those goods and services you want or need and to pay only for those you select, whether you are making arrangements when a death occurs or in advance.

The Funeral Rule, which is enforced by the Federal Trade Commission (FTC), has many provisions. These include mandated disclosures and restrictive actions. At the very start of a face-to-face discussion with the public regarding the selection of funeral goods or services and/or the prices of them, the funeral director is required to give the consumer:

- The GPL for retention upon collection and signed receipt of the Consumer Protection Fee
- The price for each item the consumer requests on dated company letterhead
- The GPL for retention, and the casket and vault price list for reference only
- The casket price list and vault price list for retention, and the GPL for reference only

The FTC's Funeral Rule helps consumers make informed decisions during very difficult times. When a loved one dies, grieving family members and friends often are confronted with dozens of decisions about the funeral – all of which must be made quickly and under great emotional duress. What kind of funeral should it be? What funeral provider should be used? Should the body be buried, cremated, or donated to science? What are consumers legally required to buy? What other arrangements should be planned? And what is it going to cost? Under the FTC's Funeral Rule, consumers have the right to get a general price list from a funeral provider when they ask about funeral arrangements. They also have the right to choose the funeral goods and services they want (with some exceptions), and funeral providers must state this right on the general price list.

If state or local law requires purchase of any particular item, the funeral provider must disclose it on the price list, with a reference to the specific law. The funeral provider may not refuse, or charge a fee, to handle a casket bought elsewhere, and a provider offering cremations must make alternative containers available.

> The Funeral Rule, which is enforced by the Federal Trade Commission (FTC), has many provisions. These include mandated disclosures and restrictive actions. At the very start of a face-to-face discussion with the public regarding the selection of funeral goods or services and/or the prices of them, the funeral director is required to give the consumer:
>
> a. The GPL for retention upon collection and signed receipt of the Consumer Protection Fee
>
> b. The price for each item the consumer requests on dated company letterhead
>
> c. The GPL for retention, and the casket and vault price list for reference only **Correct**
>
> d. The casket price list and vault price list for retention, and the GPL for reference only
>
> **The GPL for retention, and the casket and vault price list for reference only.** The General Price List (GPL) is provided to the consumer for their retention. The funeral home cannot charge the consumer for a copy of the GPL. The casket and/or vault price list need to be handed to the consumer for reference as the products and prices are discussed, but the funeral director is not required by law to distribute them for retention. The Consumer Protection Fee applies to pre-need contracts. There is no requirement to compare prices requested by the consumer on dated company letterhead.

The FTC conducts undercover inspections every year to make sure that funeral homes are complying with the agency's Funeral Rule.

The Funeral Rule applies anytime a consumer seeks information from a funeral provider, whether the consumer is asking about pre-need or at-need arrangements.

What is considered to be the cornerstone of the FTC funeral rule?

The cornerstone of the Funeral Rule is permission for embalming. For those callers phoning the funeral home inquiring about prices, you cannot require them to give their names, addresses, or phone numbers before you give them the requested information.

Which of the following is prohibited by the Funeral Rule?

The Funeral Rule prohibits funeral homes from telling consumers state or local law require embalming. If state law does require embalming, the funeral home may tell the family embalming is required under specific circumstances. Funeral homes must disclose this in writing on the General Price List.

What does the Funeral Rule require?

Under the FTC's Funeral Rule, consumers have the right to get a general price list from a funeral provider when they ask about funeral arrangements. They also have the right to choose the funeral goods and services they want (with some exceptions), and funeral providers must state this right on the general price list.

What is constructive custody of a dead human body?

While the body is in the morgue, the hospital has actual custody of the body, but the family and the funeral home each have constructive custody of the body (i.e. a right to the body even though they do not have possession of the body.)

The person with the authority and duty of final disposition who may or may not have "actual" custody (physical possession) of the deceased at a particular moment is considered to have what kind of custody?

- ○ Caveat emptor
- ○ Constructive
- ○ Consignment
- ○ Endowment

Constructive custody, Constructive possession is retained by the person with the power of disposition even when the dead body is in the actual custody of someone else.

If an individual has the paramount right of disposition, he or she is not compelled by law to share it with others. This being the case, the individual may elect to hold a private funeral and invite or exclude those whom he or she chooses. Extends even to services conducted in cemeteries.

Who is the secondary right to control final disposition of a deceased person rest with?

Significant other, friend, landlord, attorney, funeral director, accountant, etc.

If there is no Primary Party found to have the right of disposition the State is the Secondary Party with Right of Disposition and will be responsible for the final disposition.

The person with the authority and duty of final disposition who may or may not have "actual" custody (physical possession) of the deceased at a particular moment is considered to have what kind of custody?

   a. Caveat emptor

   b. Constructive `Correct`

   c. Consignment

   d. Endowment

> **Constructive.** Constructive custody in funeral service is the term applied to the custody rights that supersede actual custody rights, and they include the right of a party to control the disposition of the deceased. The person with actual custody may sometimes be a third party (such as a livery or public carrier), but someone else would maintain constructive custody at all times. Caveat emptor is Latin for "let the buyer beware." Consignment refers to merchandise shipped to an agent or to a customer. It does not take place as a result of an actual purchase, but under an agreement obliging the consignee to pay the consignor for the goods within a certain period of time once the merchandise is sold. Endowment refers to a permanent fund of property or money that is established to benefit an institution or person. An example is the sale of perpetual care cemetery property.

What are the next of kin laws in Maine?

In order to inherit under Maine's intestate succession law, the heir in question must survive the decedent by at least 120 hours. In addition, relatives conceived before you die but born after the decedent's death are eligible to inherit as if they had been born while the decedent was alive.

How long can a body stay in the morgue?

A body presents little threat to public health in the first day following the death. However, after 24 hours the body will need some level of embalming.

A mortuary will be able to preserve the body for approximately a week. Regardless of the embalming, decomposition will begin after one week.

Who has ownership of a dead body?

Who owns your body after death? The answer: no one. However, how your body is disposed is a matter for your personal representatives to decide. Controlling what happens to your body after you die may be important to you, for others, not so much.

Can a person control who comes to the funeral?

Unless the person says so, it is implied that anyone is welcome to attend the funeral. While a large funeral service is often a beautiful thing, it can also become a source of stress if there is tension among those in attendance.

Who has top priority when it comes to the right to possession of a decedent's body?

While the primary and paramount right to possession of the body and control of the burial or is vested in the surviving spouse, the right of a surviving spouse to control the burial is dependent on the peculiar circumstances of each case, and may be waived by consent or otherwise.

How long can a dead body be refrigerated?

Refrigeration is an alternative option, which lasts longer than embalming. Morticians will keep the body in a fridge at two degrees Celsius instead of preparing the body with chemicals. However, you need to keep in mind that a refrigerated corpse will only last for three to four weeks.

What's the longest you can hold a body before a funeral?

There is no legal time limit on how long you can wait to bury a body, but most funeral homes will require that the funeral takes place within 30 days.

What does a body look like after 2 weeks in a morgue?

After two weeks, the body starts to bloat and change its color to red after the blood present in the body starts to decompose. Once the corpse surpasses the fourth week, you can witness liquefaction in the rest of the remains. The teeth and nails also begin to fall during this time frame.

How long can a body be kept in a coffin before burial?

Embalming or refrigeration at the mortuary can help to preserve your loved one for some time but can't prevent nature from taking its course eventually. It's possible to delay a funeral service indefinitely but a cremation or burial shouldn't be delayed for more than four weeks after someone dies.

Insolvent Estate

After a loved one passes away, the last thing the grieving family member wants to deal with are debt collectors asking them to pay the loved one's debts.

An insolvent estate is an estate of a deceased person whose assets are insufficient to pay the estate's debts, taxes, and administrative expenses. It is the state statute that controls the priority of these claims. In most states, though, the priority of claims—from top priority to lowest—is ordered as follows:

○ Taxes, funeral expenses, and medical bills

○ Medical bills, taxes, and funeral expenses

○ Funeral expenses, administration expenses, and taxes

○ Administration expenses, funeral expenses, and taxes

So what happens with those debts after the death of a loved one?

According to the Federal Trade Commission (FTC), the nation's consumer protection agency, family members typically are not obligated to pay the debts of a deceased relative from their own assets.

Who actually is responsible for the debts then?

The estate of the deceased person actually owes the debt. If there' is not enough money in the estate, the debt typically goes unpaid. According to the FTC there are exceptions to this rule; a surviving family member may be responsible for the debt if s/he:

- Co-signed the debt obligation;
- Lives in a community property state, such as California;

- Is the deceased person's spouse and state law requires him/her to pay a type of debt, like health care expenses; or
- Was legally responsible for resolving the estate and didn't comply with certain state probate laws.

The rest of the debt obligations fall to the deceased person's estate (if there is one), and that is where the situation can get a little muddy, especially for relatives who think they are in line for an inheritance. There can only be an inheritance if there are enough assets in the estate to pay off the deceased person's debts.

> An insolvent estate is an estate of a deceased person whose assets are insufficient to pay the estate's debts, taxes, and administrative expenses. It is the state statute that controls the priority of these claims. In most states, though, the priority of claims—from top priority to lowest—is ordered as follows:
>
> a. Taxes, funeral expenses, and medical bills
>
> b. Medical bills, taxes, and funeral expenses
>
> c. Funeral expenses, administration expenses, and taxes *Correct*
>
> d. Administration expenses, funeral expenses, and taxes
>
> **Funeral expenses, administration expenses, and taxes.** In most states the funeral expenses of the deceased take top priority. This claim is immediately followed by the administration fees associated with settling the estate. Taxes come last. Taxes are not a preferred claim expense over the funeral expenses of the deceased in most states. Medical bills owed do not supersede taxes or funeral expenses in most states. Administration expenses are given less priority than funeral expenses and taxes in most states.

If one is not sure whether or not they are legally obligated to pay a deceased person's debts from their own assets, it is best to talk to a lawyer.

The FTC also explains that the executor is the person named in a will who is responsible for settling a deceased person's affairs.

Without a will in place, the court may instead appoint an administrator, personal representative, or universal successor, and give that person the authority to settle her/his loved one's affairs. In some states, others (or other people) may have that authority, even if they have not been formally appointed by the court.

If a person is the executor, it is their responsibility to figure out how to pay creditors by drawing on the money and holdings in the estate when the owner died.

It is NOT the family's responsibility to use their own money to pay off those debts (unless they are included within the four exceptions listed above).

So what happens to assets?

Not every asset someone owns is up-for-grabs upon death. The law divides the deceased person's assets into exempt and non-exempt categories, with the primary distinction being that exempt assets can't be liquidated to cover debts.

The list of exempt assets varies by state, but two major assets are exempt everywhere: retirement savings and life insurance policies. Those two particular assets can be distributed to beneficiaries regardless of debts owed by the deceased.

Assets that are non-exempt, meaning available to be liquidated and used to pay off debts, includes a houses, cars, boats, checking/savings accounts, artwork, stamp or coin collections - basically anything that has enough value to be sold.

Insolvent estates are unfortunately becoming a common feature. An insolvent estate is where the assets that remain aren't sufficient to pay funeral expenses and cover the deceased's debts and liabilities. As a result, there will be nothing for the beneficiaries of the estate to inherit.

The Federal Trade Commission (FTC)

The Federal Trade Commission is an independent agency of the United States government whose principal mission is the enforcement of civil antitrust law and the promotion of consumer protection. The FTC shares jurisdiction over federal civil antitrust law enforcement with the Justice Department Antitrust Division.

A federal government agency created to promote consumer protection, encourage free and fair competition, and prevent what regulators determine to be anti-competitive business practices is called:

○ FTC

○ ICCFA

○ OSHA

○ NFDA

The FTC was created to act as a guardian of fair markets, armed with broad authority to ensure our economy is one in which consumers, workers, and honest businesses can thrive. More specifically, the Federal Trade Commission's mission is to prevent unfair, deceptive or anticompetitive business practices. The FTC's meaning is tied to benefiting consumers and businesses while building a healthy economy.

The Federal Trade Commission (FTC) was created through the Federal Trade Commission's Act of 1914. This gave the government the authority to regulate unscrupulous acts among businesses.

The Act of 1914 provides the U.S. government with the legal tools it needs to prevent business practices that are unfair, deceptive or anti-competitive. The goal of the Act of 1914 was to create fair competition amongst businesses while protecting consumers from fraudulent businesses or business practices.

A federal government agency created to promote consumer protection, encourage free and fair competition, and prevent what regulators determine to be anti-competitive business practices is called:

a. FTC *Correct*

b. ICCFA

c. OSHA

d. NFDA

FTC. The Federal Trade Commission (FTC) is the government agency created to promote consumer protection and fair competition, and also to prevent anti-competitive commerce practices. The ICCFA is a national trade association for funeral homes and cemeteries, and serves as a resource for cemetery/funeral service professionals and the public. OSHA is the Occupational Safety Health Administration, and is a government agency created to prevent work-related injuries, illnesses, and fatalities by issuing and enforcing standards for workplace safety and health. The NFDA is the National Funeral Directors Association. It is not a government agency but a trade association for funeral directors. It serves as a resource for funeral service professionals and the public.

What does the Federal Trade Commission (FTC) do?

The FTC was created in 1914 by President Woodrow Wilson with the goal of protecting consumers, investors and businesses from anti-competitive practices. A significant aspect of the FTC is to prevent monopolies and protect consumers by putting a stop to fraudulent companies.

For instance, you witness the FTC in action every time an influencer discloses that they have been paid to promote a product or a service. The FTC is also responsible for guarding against false advertising and enforcing full disclosure requirements.

The FTC was created to enforce provisions in two other acts as well, those being the 1980 Sherman Antitrust Act and the 1914 Clayton Antitrust Act. The FTC stands for consumers and antitrust laws that prioritize the promotion of equitable business across the board.

In doing so, the FTC investigates fraud, makes congressional inquiries, gives companies pre-merger notifications and protects consumer rights. The FTC also works against anything that is viewed as anti-competitive behavior.

The FTC is an investigative authority, meaning the FTC can investigate any instance of behavior that is perceived as contradicting the rules set forth by the FTC. Under its investigative authority, the FTC may also collaborate with international or foreign antitrust authorities, according to mutual or bilateral agreements under the International Antitrust Enforcement Assistance Act.

The FTC is also an enforcement authority that functions for the sake of consumer protection while enforcing domestic antitrust laws via the Bureau of Competition. Additionally, the FTC may create rules that address unfair or deceptive methods of competition that are commonplace, including unfair and deceptive advertising protocols or business methods.

Tort

A tort is a civil wrong that causes a claimant to suffer loss or harm, resulting in legal liability for the person who commits the tortious act.

Tort law can be contrasted with criminal law, which deals with criminal wrongs that are punishable by the state. While criminal law aims to punish individuals who commit crimes, tort law aims to compensate individuals who suffer harm as a result of the actions of others.

Some wrongful acts, such as assault and battery, can result in both a civil lawsuit and a criminal prosecution in countries where the civil and criminal legal systems are separate. Tort law may also be contrasted with contract law, which provides civil remedies after breach of a duty that arises from a contract. Obligations in both tort and criminal law are more fundamental and are imposed regardless of whether the parties have a contract.

> A wrongful act by a person for which damages can be sought by the injured party through a civil lawsuit is called a:
>
> ○ Tort
>
> ○ Mutilation
>
> ○ Obstruction
>
> ○ Replevin

While tort law in civil law jurisdictions largely derives from Roman law, common law jurisdictions derive their tort law from customary English tort law. In civil law jurisdictions based on civil codes, both contractual and tortious liability is typically outlined in a civil code based on Roman Law principles.

There are three categories of torts:

- Intentional torts,
- Negligence, and
- Strict liability torts.

A wrongful act by a person for which damages can be sought by the injured party through a civil lawsuit is called a:

a. Tort `Correct`

b. Mutilation

c. Obstruction

d. Replevin

> **Tort.** A tort occurs when a person takes a wrongful action against another person or property, and is a civil law matter. Mutilation as it relates to mortuary science is inflicting bodily damage or injury on a person or animal by removing or destroying body parts. Obstruction occurs when a person or a situation creates an impasse or hinders someone from doing something. Replevin is an action to pick up goods or property by somebody who claims to own them and who promises to have the claim later tested in court. It does not apply to human remains.

Intentional torts

Intentional torts involve situations in which the defendant desires or knows to a substantial certainty that his act will cause the plaintiff damage. They include battery, assault, false imprisonment, intentional infliction of emotional distress, trespass to land, trespass to chattels, conversion, invasion of privacy, malicious prosecution, abuse of process, fraud, inducing breach of contract, intentional interference with business relations, and defamation of character (libel/slander).

Negligence

Amongst unintentional torts one finds negligence as being the most common source of common law. Most Americans are under the impression that most people can sue for any type of negligence, but it is untrue in most US jurisdictions (partly because negligence is one of the few torts for which ordinary people can and do obtain liability insurance.)

Some jurisdictions recognize one or more designations less than actual intentional wrongdoing, but more egregious than mere negligence, such as "wanton", "reckless" or "despicable" conduct. A finding in those states that a defendant's conduct was "wanton," "reckless" or "despicable", rather than merely negligent, can be significant because certain defenses, such as contributory negligence, are often unavailable when such conduct is the cause of the damages.

Strict liability

Strict liability torts are brought for injuries resulting from ultra-hazardous activities, for which the defendant will be held liable even if there was no negligence on his/her part. Strict liability also applies to some types of product liability claims and to copyright infringement and some trademark cases. Some statutory torts are also strict liability, including many environmental torts.

The Power of the Government

Police Power is the inherent power and constitutional authority of the government to adopt and enforce regulations and laws to promote public health, safety, morals, and general welfare of its citizens, which includes the control of public land use.

> The power of a government to impose what it considers reasonable restrictions and laws on its citizens for the maintenance of public safety, health, order, and welfare is called:
>
> ○ Tort
>
> ○ Police power
>
> ○ Restrictive covenant
>
> ○ Uniform probate code

In United States constitutional law, the police power is the capacity of the states to regulate behavior and enforce order within their territory for the betterment of the health, safety, morals, and general welfare of their inhabitants. As part of their sovereign powers, states possess the power to regulate private activities in order to protect or promote public order, health, safety, morals, and general welfare.

State police powers gives states the authority to prescribe reasonable laws necessary to preserve the public order, health, safety, welfare, and morals within the limits of the state and federal constitutions. The Centers for Disease Control and Prevention (CDC) leads efforts to control communicable disease outbreaks and promote mass immunization. The federal government also assists states with funding (when state resources are not available) and guidance for work such as emergency preparedness.

Because the market alone cannot ensure all Americans access to quality health care, the government must preserve the interests of its citizens by supplementing the market where there are gaps and regulating the market where there is inefficiency or unfairness.

The power of a government to impose what it considers reasonable restrictions and laws on its citizens for the maintenance of public safety, health, order, and welfare is called:

a. Tort

b. Police power **Correct**

c. Restrictive covenant

d. Uniform probate code

> **Police power.** Police power is based on constitutional law, and is the ability of the federal government and the states to order and be in command of certain prescribed legal actions necessary for the maintenance of public safety, health, order, and welfare. A tort is a wrongful action against a person or property, and is a civil law matter. A restrictive covenant is a deed restriction restraining the use of property in some prescribed manner. Uniform probate code is a statute passed by many states to varying degrees that spells out the laws that exist regarding the affairs of decedents and their estates.

The Constitution protects property rights through the Fifth and Fourteenth Amendments' Due Process Clauses and, more directly, through the Fifth Amendment's Takings Clause: "nor shall private property be taken for public use without just compensation."

Constitution allocates public health powers among the federal government and the states. Federal public health powers include the authority to tax, spend, and regulate interstate commerce.

Memorial service

A funeral service and a memorial service both serve the same purpose – they are the ritual through which we formerly say goodbye to our departed loved one. Both can be as long or short as required and focus on being a tribute and celebration of the life of the person who departed.

Which of the following funeral rites is conducted without the presence of the casketed body?

○ Entombment service

○ Memorial service

○ Graveside service

○ Traditional or complete cremation service

A Funeral Service

A funeral service typically takes place with the body of the departed present, whereas a memorial service takes place without the actual body present.

A funeral service can refer to a traditional graveside burial service, or it can refer to a funeral service conducted in a chapel when cremation is later performed. A funeral service is most often conducted within a week of the death occurring.

A Memorial Service

A memorial service generally takes place sometime after the death and disposition have occurred.

It is usually a service specifically to memorialize the life of the deceased. If cremation has been performed, often a memorial service is conducted to inter or scatter the cremated remains at the same time as the celebration of the deceased's life.

Which of the following funeral rites is conducted without the presence of the casketed body?

a. Entombment service

b. Memorial service **Correct**

c. Graveside service

d. Traditional or complete cremation service

Memorial service. A memorial service is always held without the casketed body. Funeral rite is a term that can describe both funerals and/or memorial services. Funeral, on the other hand, describes a service conducted when the body is present. During an entombment service, the human casketed body is placed in a crypt. A graveside service refers to one in which the deceased is in a casket. It is held at the cemetery interment site (grave) instead of a church or chapel. The casketed body is present at a traditional or complete cremation service, but at the end of the service the decreased goes to the crematory to be cremated instead of to the cemetery for interment burial.

A memorial service can also be held following a private family funeral service to enable extended attendance for the purpose of memorialization of the deceased.

Sometimes the family will arrange a private family funeral service and then hold a memorial service at a later date when the family and friends who could not attend the funeral can gather.

A memorial service is often held when someone had particular ties to a community as a ritual to help people pay their last respects.

How you decide to memorialize your loved one should be an entirely personal choice, and observing the wishes of the deceased. We often hear the quote that "funerals are for the living," which, of course, they are. But too often, families are swayed into a funeral service that can become overwhelming, driven by our social concerns with what other people will think.

The funeral industry today has evolved to such a scale as to make the whole 'service' aspect of a funeral largely an aspect that is in their domain.

Veterans and the U.S. Department of Veterans Affairs (VA)

The VA will furnish a burial flag for memorialization for each other than dishonorable discharged. 2. Who Is Eligible to Receive the Burial Flag? Generally, the flag is given to the next-of-kin, as a keepsake, after its use during the funeral service.

> A deceased veteran or reservist who was entitled to receive retired military pay qualifies to receive an American flag after the completion and submittal of the APPLICATION FOR UNITED STATES FLAG FOR BURIAL PURPOSES form, also known as:
>
> ○ VA Form 21-530
>
> ○ SSA-721
>
> ○ VA form 27-2008
>
> ○ VA form 40-1330

Why Does VA Provide a Burial Flag?

A United States flag is provided, at no cost, to drape the casket or accompany the urn of a deceased Veteran who served honorably in the U.S. Armed Forces. It is furnished to honor the memory of a Veteran's military service to his or her country. VA will furnish a burial flag for memorialization for each other than dishonorable discharged.

- Veteran who served during wartime
- Veteran who died on active duty after May 27, 1941
- Veteran who served after January 31, 1955
- Peacetime Veteran who was discharged or released before June 27, 1950
- Certain persons who served in the organized military forces of the Commonwealth of the Philippines while in service of the U.S Armed forces and who died on or after April 25, 1951
- Certain former members of the Selected Reserves

Who Is Eligible to Receive the Burial Flag?

Generally, the flag is given to the next-of-kin, as a keepsake, after its use during the funeral service. When there is no next-of-kin, VA will furnish the flag to a friend making request for it. For those VA national cemeteries with an Avenue of Flags, families of Veterans buried in these national cemeteries may donate the burial flags of their loved ones to be flown on patriotic holidays.

A deceased veteran or reservist who was entitled to receive retired military pay qualifies to receive an American flag after the completion and submittal of the APPLICATION FOR UNITED STATES FLAG FOR BURIAL PURPOSES form, also known as:

a. VA Form 21-530

b. SSA-721

c. VA form 27-2008 **Correct**

d. VA form 40-1330

> **VA form 27-2008.** The APPLICATION FOR UNITED STATES FLAG FOR BURIAL PURPOSES, also known as VA form 27-2008, is the accepted document to apply for an American flag. The APPLICATION FOR BURIAL BENEFITS is the form to apply for burial benefits at the Veterans Administration. The STATEMENT OF DEATH BY FUNERAL DIRECTOR is a form completed by the funeral director to notify the Social Security Administration of the death. It is unrelated to the Veterans Administration. The APPLICATION FOR STANDARD GOVERNMENT HEADSTONE OR MARKER is for a memorial issued by the Veterans Administration.

How to Apply?

A person may apply for the flag by completing VA Form 27-2008, Application for United States Flag for Burial Purposes. They may get a flag at any U.S. Post Office or VA regional office. Generally, the funeral director will help you obtain the flag.

Can a Burial Flag Be Replaced?

The law allows us to issue one flag for a Veteran's funeral. They cannot replace it if it is lost, destroyed, or stolen. However, some Veterans' organizations or other community groups may be able to help you get another flag.

How Should the Burial Flag Be Displayed?

The proper way to display the flag depends upon whether the casket is open or closed. The instructions on VA Form 27-2008 does provide the correct method for displaying and folding the flag. The burial flag is not suitable for outside display because of its size and fabric. It is made of cotton and can easily be damaged by weather.

For more information, call (800) 827-1000 or visit the National Cemetery Administration's web site.

What if more than one family member wants a flag?

Only one flag may be issued to the family member or friend identified on the VA Form 27-2008, Application for United State Burial Flag. Only one application may be completed for each deceased Veteran.

Where can we purchase flags commercially?

A number of companies manufacture flags to the general specifications for VA burial flags and the VA may not endorse a particular manufacturer nor be held responsible for the quality or correctness of a commercially purchased flag. VA Flags are manufactured to stringent standards using 100% US materials and construction.

Who may complete a Flag Application?

A flag may be issued to a funeral director or anyone else who certifies by signature the eligibility of the deceased Veteran even if requested eligibility documentation is not attached.

How Can the Funeral Director help the VA and the Veteran?

Complete the Flag Application as completely as possible with all available information requested on the form and turn in the application to the post office as soon as possible following the death of the Veteran. The information provided helps the VA in the death notification process, easing the burden on family members as well as authorizing the post office to order a replacement flag ensuring availability to the funeral director for future requirements.

If given a defective flag, what do we do?

Return the flag to the post office from which it was received. The post office may replace the flag with another and return the defective flag to the VA for replacement.

If the post office either doesn't have flags or has a difficult time keeping enough on hand. What can be done?

Ask the post office to contact the USPS Material Distribution Center at the phone number or email account listed below and an MDC Service Representative will ensure the post office is resupplied with sufficient flags to meet their needs. The VA does not supply flags directly to a funeral home but will always respond to calls or questions to ensure that burial flags are always available.

Where can I get VA Form 27-2008, Application for United States Burial Flag?

The current Flag Application is dated July 2012 and is available for downloading at http://www.vba.va.gov/pubs/forms/VBA-27-2008-ARE.pdf.

Mortuary Cots

The casket industry originated in the 1800s when local funeral directors, then known as undertakers or morticians, often operated a local furniture store and built caskets as needed for the families they serviced. A simple pine coffin in 1840 cost between $2 and $3 (between $40 and $60 in today's currency adjusted for inflation).

A portable stretcher used by both ambulances and funeral homes to move the injured or deceased that is considered to be the most important item for transferring remains from a house or an institution is called a:

○ Cot

○ Flexible stretcher

○ Transfer vehicle

○ Church truck

The problem of transferring a body of patient from a bed was a constant problem for the funeral director. Dick Ferneau came up with the idea of an elevating cot to ease the transfer of a body or patient from a home bed to a cot.

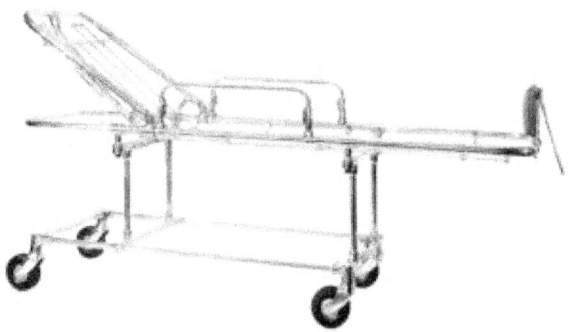

It wasn't long until the demand for a cot to elevate to the height of a hospital emergency room stretcher was recognized.

It was easier to transfer a patient from the home bed down to the low standard cot. Throughout the 1950s the evolution of EMS as a profession emerged, and the funeral director was less involved in the transport of emergency patients; although many retained the capacity to transport invalid patients.

A portable stretcher used by both ambulances and funeral homes to move the injured or deceased that is considered to be the most important item for transferring remains from a house or an institution is called a:

a. Cot **Correct**

b. Flexible stretcher

c. Transfer vehicle

d. Church truck

> **Cot.** The mortuary or ambulance cot is the most important item for transferring remains, and is a portable stretcher that has wheels, a mattress, and belts. It is used by both ambulances and funeral homes to move the injured and deceased. The flexible stretcher refers to the collapsible stretcher that folds so it can be carried up and down stairs. It can then be opened on site. The deceased can be placed on it and strapped in until they can be transferred to the cot. It is not the most important item for transfer since it is only used in special circumstances when access is difficult, such as in stairwells or elevators. The transfer vehicle refers to the actual motorized vehicle that transports the deceased from the place of death to the funeral home. The church truck is the portable device on wheels that can be extended to serve as a resting apparatus to display or move a casket in church or a funeral home.

The demand for the combination hearse ambulance custom coach was declining due to the changing user base and the economics of building the EMS industry. Demographics shaped the type of service that evolved, as many of the volunteer services started or grew, fire departments became involved, and municipal ambulance services started, as well as many private ambulance services. With the changing marketplace, the vehicles also changed with the advent of the station wagon and suburban-type trucks, and ultimately the "box" or modular ambulance.

The station wagon ambulance was the cheap and fast way to get into the ambulance service business. With that trend the need for different types of ambulance cots was immediate, as it was difficult to treat a heart patient in the low headroom of the station wagon.

Death Certificates

The death certificate verifies that the disposition of remains is done correctly and that the person being interred or cremated is the one who died. If a person live in Texas, however, the funeral home is permitted to bury someone who has died before the doctor signs the death certificate.

> **Which of the following accurately describe the purposes of a death certificate?**
> I. Shows vital statistics and cause of death for medical or actuarial research
> II. Is the legal permanent record of the deceased
> III. Is the legal document issued by the proper government agency authorizing the transportation and/or disposition of human remains
> IV. Is the legal record that final disposition has occurred
>
> ○ I, II, and IV
>
> ○ II and IV
>
> ○ I and II
>
> ○ All of the above

Louisiana law provides that the last physician to attend a decedent within 10 days of death must complete and execute a death certificate within 24 hours of death.

The executor or administrator of the decedent's estate, will need the death certificate for probate purposes. Financial institutions, like the decedent's bank or investment firms, for handling the deceased's accounts. Insurance companies, to process any life insurance claims.

What are the 3 possible manners of death on a death certificate?

The classifications are natural, accident, suicide, homicide, undetermined, and pending. Only the medical examiners and coroners may use all of the manners of death.

The death certificate declares the cause of death, location of death, time of death and some other personal information about the deceased.

Which of the following accurately describe the purposes of a death certificate?
I. Shows vital statistics and cause of death for medical or actuarial research
II. Is the legal permanent record of the deceased
III. Is the legal document issued by the proper government agency authorizing the transportation and/or disposition of human remains
IV. Is the legal record that final disposition has occurred

a. I, II, and IV **Correct**

b. II and IV

c. I and II

d. All of the above

---

i, ii, and iv. The purpose of the death certificate is to show vital statistics information and cause of death for medical or actuarial study, to serve as the legal permanent record of the deceased, and to serve as the legal record that final disposition has occurred. The Burial Cremation or Transit/Disposition Permit is a legal document issued by the proper government bureau authorizing transportation and/or disposition of human remains. It is the legal permit for the final disposition to take place.

When a death occurs, a physician or medical examiner must fill out a death certificate. In order to properly complete this document, they must determine three things: the cause, the mechanism, and the manner of death.

How long does it take to determine cause of death?

Autopsy reports are usually completed within 60 days from the date of autopsy; however, there are cases which can take 90 days or longer depending on the complexity of the case.

Who pays for an autopsy when someone dies?

Unless ordered by the state, families are required to pay for an autopsy. It's important to note that medical insurance does not cover this procedure.

The Funeral Procession

Funeral Procession is also known as a funeral cortege. A traditional funeral procession will begin at the funeral home or at the home of the person who has passed away. It can sometimes include two stages; this is often the case if the funeral service and the committal are being held at separate venues.

A typical funeral cortege would be arranged in the following order:

- ○ Lead car, hearse, clergy, pallbearers, family cars/limo, and procession
- ○ Lead car, hearse, pallbearers, clergy, family cars/limo, and procession
- ○ Hearse, lead car, clergy, pallbearers, family cars/limo, and procession
- ○ Lead car, clergy, pallbearers, hearse, family cars/limo, and procession

The funeral procession is a tradition extending back to ancient times. In the Roman Empire, it was a critical, and often dramatic, part of the funeral rites. The deceased was carried on a bed-like tray from their home to wherever they would be buried, or to the funeral pyre, if they opted for cremation.

The purpose of a funeral procession is to give a final goodbye to the deceased and provide them with a dignified burial. They are held directly after the funeral reception and takes place directly before laying the deceased in their final resting place.

The processional is led by the officiant and is followed by the pallbearers who carry the casket. Next, the family and kin to the deceased walk down the aisle, followed by close friends as they take their seats in the first few rows. A funeral recessional marks the end of the funeral service.

Vehicles taking part in a funeral procession have the right-of-way, and if you interfere, obstruct, or interrupt the funeral procession, you are subject to a citation.

> A typical funeral cortege would be arranged in the following order:
>
> a. Lead car, hearse, clergy, pallbearers, family cars/limo, and procession
>
> b. Lead car, hearse, pallbearers, clergy, family cars/limo, and procession
>
> c. Hearse, lead car, clergy, pallbearers, family cars/limo, and procession
>
> d. Lead car, clergy, pallbearers, hearse, family cars/limo, and procession *Correct*
>
> **Lead car, clergy, pallbearers, hearse, family cars/limo, and procession.** Although some states may have requirements for processions to have a police car in the lead, the order of the cortege is typically: lead car, clergy, pallbearers, hearse, family cars/limo, and procession.

If there are many cars in the procession, the attendant may place the flag on every other vehicle or every 3rd vehicle. You will also be instructed to turn your headlights on for the drive to the cemetery. Both the funeral flags and the headlights signifies to other motorists that you are part of a funeral procession.

The funeral procession usually takes place after the memorial service. It consists of a select group of people usually driving, but sometimes walking, from the service to the burial site, usually headed by a hearse carrying the coffin.

The Funeral Home

The oldest funeral home in the United States began in 1759 in Williamsburg, Virginia, started by cabinet manufacturer Anthony Hay who made coffins as a side line. Prior to the mid 1800's, women were in charge of preparing the deceased. Funeral homes came into their own as formally recognized societal institutions at a time when the funeral home industry was about to decline. In the last years of the 19th century and the first years of the 20th century, the number of funeral homes increased rapidly.

The entryway, foyer, or lobby to a funeral home or church is also called the:

- ○ Narthex
- ○ Nave
- ○ Niche
- ○ Sanctuary

The narthex is a transitional space located at the entrance of a church, cathedral, or funeral home. It serves as a vestibule or antechamber, connecting the outside world with the sacred space of the church. The narthex is typically a rectangular or square-shaped area, and may be separated from the nave by a screen or partition. It is often used as a gathering space for worshippers before and after services, and may contain artwork, statues, or other decorative elements. In some churches, the narthex may also contain a baptismal font or other religious artifacts.

The terms narthex and vestibule are used almost interchangeably, but there is a slight technical difference. A vestibule is a passage, hall, or room between the outer door and the interior of a building, whereas the narthex is a porch or lobby that connects the outside to the main worship area.

The entryway, foyer, or lobby to a funeral home or church is also called the:

a. Narthex **Correct**

b. Nave

c. Niche

d. Sanctuary

> **Narthex.** The narthex is the entryway to the funeral home or church, and is also known as the lobby or foyer. The nave is the seating or audience section of the church. A niche is a permanent resting place for cremated remains typically found in a church or cemetery. A sanctuary is the area in the church where the public are seated during the service, and can also describe the area around the altar.

In many Catholic Church buildings, there are also areas which are called by the pastor or parishioners the "narthex" or the "vestibule." While most people use these terms interchangeably, they were originally separate architectural spaces with different functions.

Why is the narthex important?

The narthex is a place of welcome — a threshold between the congregation's space and the outside environment. It helps believers to make the transition from everyday life to the celebration of the liturgy, and after the liturgy, it helps them return to daily life to live out the mystery that has been celebrated.

Sacrament of the Sick

In the Sacrament of the Sick, the person who is ill or suffering is anointed. Anointing with oil is intended to strengthen the sick person. The person may be strengthened to face the illness or surgery. The person might also be strengthened to face death.

> In the Roman Catholic faith, an anointing ceremony by a priest for the seriously ill to bring healing or for those who are dying to prepare their souls for eternity is called:

○ Paschal Candle Service

○ Sacrament of the Sick

○ Rosary Service

○ Rosary Beads

By the sacred anointing of the sick and the prayer of the priests the whole Church commends those who are ill to the suffering and glorified Lord, that he may raise them up and save them.

The Sacrament of the Sick has been known by four different names throughout history:

- Last Rites
- Extreme Unction
- Viaticum
- The Sacrament of the Sick

A Sacrament is a visible sign of God's presence, God's activity in our lives, in the Church and in our world. But it goes beyond that! Sacraments not only show us what God is like and what God dreams for us; Sacraments also make that happen!

Last Rites

Sacrament is often called "The Last Rites." It is often one of the last rituals celebrated with a person as he or she nears death.

> In the Roman Catholic faith, an anointing ceremony by a priest for the seriously ill to bring healing or for those who are dying to prepare their souls for eternity is called:
>
> a. Paschal Candle Service
>
> b. Sacrament of the Sick **Correct**
>
> c. Rosary Service
>
> d. Rosary Beads

> **Sacrament of the Sick.** The Sacrament of the Sick is an anointing ritual conducted by a priest. Catholics believe it is a rite in which God can help cure the critically ill or help prepare the souls of those who are dying for eternity. The Paschal candle is a large, white candle used in the Western rites of Christianity (Roman Catholic, Anglican, Lutheran, etc.). It is positioned near the casket during funeral masses. A Rosary Service is a sequence of Roman Catholic prayers. Rosary Beads, which consist of a string of beads and a crucifix, are used to count the prayers said during a Rosary Service.

What God wants to accomplish in this Sacrament is strengthening and healing.

Viaticum

A third name sometimes given to this Sacrament is "Viaticum." "Viaticum" means "Food for the Journey."

Traditionally, one of the "Last Rites" is giving the dying person Communion. If the Sacrament is called "Viaticum," you are recognizing that the Eucharist is indeed food for that final journey home to God; it may also be food to sustain the person on the road of returning to health and wholeness.

Sacrament of the Sick

If the Sacrament is called the "Sacrament of the Sick," then you have the focus more clearly. The Sacrament is really about what God wants to do in us and through us and for us in this wonderful encounter.

It tells us that God is love, and love is always oriented toward healing and wholeness. God dreams that we might all be one, whole and live a life not touched by death. Sickness is not part of God's will for humanity. Sickness and death came into the world with sin. If you face illness, God walks with us every step of the way, and sustains us and strengthens us with the Sacraments and through the love and concern of family, friends and health care professionals.

God's will is that all people will be healed and reconciled with one another and with God.

The Holy Communion

Holy Communion, also known as the Lord's Supper, is taken in remembrance of what Jesus has done for humanity. The bread represents Jesus' body that was scourged and broken before and during His crucifixion, and the cup represents His shed blood.

The name for the sanctified elements of Holy Communion that comprise the essential rudiments for liturgical worship is:

○ Paschal Candle

○ Communion Paten

○ Eucharist

○ Trisagion

Jesus implemented Holy Communion through the last supper He shared with His disciples. He took bread and, when He had broken it, said, "This is my body which is for you. Do this in remembrance of me."

In the same way, He also took the cup, after supper, saying, "This cup is the new covenant in my blood. Do this, as often as you drink, in remembrance of me. For as often as you eat this bread and drink this cup, you proclaim the Lord's death until He comes."

At the cross, God took all of our sicknesses and diseases and put them on Jesus' originally perfect and healthy body, so that we can walk in divine health. The Bible says by His stripes, we are healed.

Isaiah 53:5, "But He was pierced for our rebellion, crushed for our sins. He was beaten so we could be made whole. He was whipped so we could be healed."

Peter 2:24, "He personally carried our sins in His body on the cross so that we can be dead to sin and live what is right. By His wounds, you are healed."

What is the meaning of the Eucharist?

The word "Eucharist" refers to the Sacrament of the Eucharist, which is the Body and Blood of Jesus truly present on the altar under the appearances of bread and wine.

> The name for the sanctified elements of Holy Communion that comprise the essential rudiments for liturgical worship is:
>
> a. Paschal Candle
>
> b. Communion Paten
>
> c. Eucharist [Correct]
>
> d. Trisagion

> **Eucharist.** The Eucharist is the name for the sanctified elements of Holy Communion, which comprise the essential rudiments for liturgical worship. The Paschal Candle is a large, white candle used in the Western rites of Christianity (Roman Catholic, Anglican, Lutheran, etc.) that is placed near the casket during funeral masses. The Communion Paten is a saucer-shaped plate usually made of precious metal that is held under the chin of the communicant to catch any particle of the Sacred Host that may fall. It is similar to the Mass Paten, but has a handle that projects outward. The Trisagion is the name for the three short blessings that are part of the funeral rites of the Eastern Orthodox faith.

What is the difference between Holy Communion and Eucharist?

The Holy Eucharist, then, refers to the whole action of the Mass, including its sacrificial nature. Holy Communion refers to one aspect of that action: the reception of the Body and Blood of the Lord.

Is the Eucharist only Catholic?

Only those Churches whose bishops were ordained in an unbroken historical line back to the apostles can claim to have the valid sacrament of Orders, with its three levels of bishop, priest, and deacon. Therefore, only those Churches (i.e. Catholic and Orthodox) have the valid Eucharist as Christ intended.

Why is the Holy Eucharist so important?

The Eucharist is the center of Catholic faith. By receiving the Holy Eucharist, they remember the sacrifice Jesus Christ made. Jesus commanded us to love, to remember Him, and to wait for His return. We do these things by receiving His Body and Blood.

Is the Eucharist just the bread?

Just one-third of U.S. Catholics agree with their church that Eucharist is body, blood of Christ. Transubstantiation – the idea that during Mass, the bread and wine used for Communion become the body and blood of Jesus Christ – is central to the Catholic faith.

The FCC and the Declining Price Model

A price determination method whereby the casket wholesale cost is multiplied by a factor that decreases as the wholesale cost increases; i.e. cheaper units are marked up by a higher factor than more expensive units.

> Which of the following statements concerning the merchandise pricing strategy known as the Declining Price Structure Model is correct?
>
> ○ Creates a lower margin on the less expensive caskets
>
> ○ Creates a lower margin on the most expensive caskets
>
> ○ Encourages the consumer to buy better merchandise since the CVI improves with higher-priced caskets
>
> ○ Both b and c

Using the Modified Declining Price method provides for a reduced markup on the low-end casket thus providing an option for families to purchase lower-priced caskets.

You are a funeral provider if you sell or offer to sell funeral goods and both types of funeral services. You do not have to be a licensed funeral director and your business does not have to be a licensed funeral home to be covered by the FCC Funeral Rule. Cemeteries, crematories, and other businesses can also be "funeral providers" if they market both funeral goods and services.

You must comply with the Rule even if a particular consumer buys only goods or only funeral services, but not both. If you offer to sell both goods and services, you must comply with the Rule for every customer. However, you are not covered by the Rule if you sell only funeral goods, such as caskets, but not services relating to the disposition of remains.

Unless state or local law requires embalming, you may not tell consumers that embalming is required for practical purposes in the following situations:

- When the consumer wants a direct cremation;

- When the consumer wants an immediate burial; or

- When refrigeration is available and the consumer wants a closed-casket funeral with no formal viewing or visitation.

> Which of the following statements concerning the merchandise pricing strategy known as the Declining Price Structure Model is correct?
>
> a. Creates a lower margin on the less expensive caskets
>
> b. Creates a lower margin on the most expensive caskets
>
> c. Encourages the consumer to buy better merchandise since the CVI improves with higher-priced caskets
>
> d. Both b and c **Correct**
>
> ---
>
> **Both B: and C:** The Declining Price Structure Model incorporates a lower margin on higher-priced caskets so the consumer CVI improves as they spend more. Both B: and C: are components of the Declining Price Structure Model. The Modified Declining Model places a lower margin on less expensive caskets.

Example 1: A family wants to arrange a funeral with a formal viewing. The funeral will take place three days after death has occurred on a hot summer day. Your state does not require embalming. You do not have refrigeration facilities. In this situation, you can tell the family that the funeral home requires embalming as a practical necessity to delay decomposition of the remains and to preserve them for viewing. You may not tell the family that the law requires embalming in this case because that is not true.

Example 2: A family wants to arrange an immediate burial, but does not want to pay for embalming. Embalming is not required by your state law. Before burial takes place, one family member wants to look briefly at the deceased by lifting the lid of the casket. Here, you may not tell the family that embalming is required. The request to see the deceased does not constitute a formal viewing.

In situations like the Example 2, you also cannot require the family to pay for "other preparation of the body," if they decline embalming.

Types of Caskets

Caskets can be categorized into two basic material types. Those manufactured out of a variety of metal materials including Bronze, Copper, Stainless Steel, and Standard Steel and those crafted out of a variety of wood materials including Mahogany, Walnut, Cherry, Maple, Oak, Pine, Poplar and Veneer.

A casket constructed of various tree species such as salix, poplar, or cottonwood is called:

○ Single hinged panel

○ Wood veneer

○ Selected hardwood

○ Pine box

Metal caskets constructed from Bronze and Copper offer permanent non-rusting materials, which have been used for centuries for sculptures and monuments and are considered to be the highest quality available in metal caskets and present a most prestigious statement. The most significant feature difference between metal and wood caskets lies in how the lid closes against the shell of the casket. In the majority of metal caskets, a rubber gasket is inserted and wrapped around the entire perimeter of the casket shell. When the lid of the casket is closed a sealing key is inserted on the exterior foot end of the casket and turned to provide a secure closure. The gasket feature has been designed to prevent outside elements from entering the casket in the burial state. The gasketed seal in no way prevents or slows down the naturally occurring decomposition of the body. The gasketed feature is exclusive to most metal caskets. Wood caskets are not constructed with gaskets.

The most economical metal caskets are made from standard steel sometimes referred to as carbon steel. This is a strong and durable metal, which is used to build everything from automobiles to skyscrapers.

Like furniture, wood caskets are available in a variety of types and finishes from magnificent highly polished cherry finishes to natural satin-finished oak grains.

A casket constructed of various tree species such as salix, poplar, or cottonwood is called:

a. Single hinged panel

b. Wood veneer

c. Selected hardwood **Correct**

d. Pine box

Selected hardwood. Selected hardwood is a phrase used to describe a casket made of various trees, such as salix, poplar, or cottonwood. Single hinged panel refers to a casket lid that is in two sections. Wood veneer refers to the method of using glue during assembly to join a thin layer of superior wood to a layer of less costly wood so the superior wood is on top. A pine box is a casket made of wood from a pine tree.

Mahogany, Walnut, and Cherry are considered to be among the most elegantly crafted wood caskets and offer exquisite highly polished finishes similar to the finest furniture along with classical urn and rounded corner shell designs adding softness to the casket exterior appearance.

There are various types of casket interior styles. In one style, the lining material is placed on a metal form. Weights are added, and the material is then steamed and attached to an upholstery or backing. This interior style is known as:

○ Masselin

○ Crushed

○ Extendover

○ Tufted

Caskets crafted from Maple and Oak are woods everyone is familiar with. Maple has amazing strength and hardness and anyone who has ever gone bowling has walked on maple. Oak is noted for its highly recognizable graining pattern which is a predominant reason families select oak caskets.

There are various types of casket interior styles. In one style, the lining material is placed on a metal form. Weights are added, and the material is then steamed and attached to an upholstery or backing. This interior style is known as:

a. Masselin

b. Crushed **Correct**

c. Extendover

d. Tufted

Crushed. Casket interiors featuring a crushed style have a lining fabric placed on a metal form. Weights are added, and the material is then steamed and attached to an upholstery or backing. Masselin is the paper used in layers of sheets that is pressed and made up to provide an upholstery or backing. The extendover is the segment of the casket interior that extends over the top body molding. A tufted casket interior is made by inserting a padded material between a lining material and a backing material. Stitches are then added to create raised puffs.

Caskets use various lining materials. One material is a thin, crinkled cloth made of silk, cotton, rayon, or wool called:

○ Crepe

○ Satin

○ Velvet

○ Linen

Caskets use various lining materials. One material is a thin, crinkled cloth made of silk, cotton, rayon, or wool called:

a. Crepe **Correct**

b. Satin

c. Velvet

d. Linen

Crepe. Crepe is a lightweight fabric lining cloth that has a slim, daintily crinkled or ridged facade made of silk, cotton, rayon, or wool. Satin is a fabric made of woven silk, nylon, or rayon that has a smooth, silky face. Velvet is a fabric made of woven silk, cotton, or rayon that has an evenly distributed, short, substantial, and dense pile. It is typically found in costlier caskets. Linen is a fabric made from the flax plant or non-flax fibers that are woven into a cross-section contour that contributes to the coarse consistency of the fabric.

What is the difference between a cenotaph and a memorial?

A cenotaph, is simply a memorial, headstone, or marker honoring a decedent who is buried elsewhere. ' Cenotaphs typically take on the characteristics of the memorials in any given cemetery section. They can be constructed of Granite or Bronze and they can honor a single individual or multiple individuals together.

> A monument that is erected to the memory of the dead but may not serve as the physical resting place for the deceased is called a:
>
> ○ Cenotaph
>
> ○ Crypt
>
> ○ Epitaph
>
> ○ Columbarium

One of the best examples of a cenotaph is appropriately called The Cenotaph. It can be found on Whitehall, a street in Westminster located in central London. The Cenotaph in London is designated as the official national war memorial for all of the United Kingdom.

What is an empty grave called?

Cenotaph - a grave where the body is not present; a memorial erected as over a grave, but at a place where the body has not been interred. A cenotaph may look exactly like any other grave in terms of marker and inscription.

A monument that is erected to the memory of the dead but may not serve as the physical resting place for the deceased is called a:

a. Cenotaph [Correct]

b. Crypt

c. Epitaph

d. Columbarium

Cenotaph. A cenotaph is a headstone or a commemorative plaque dedicated to deceased persons that are frequently interred in another location, such as the Vietnam War Memorial in Washington or at a cemetery's scattering garden for cremated remains. A crypt is a chamber in a mausoleum that is generally large enough to hold the casketed remains of one or several deceased persons. An epitaph is an inscribed message found on a monument describing the deeds or traits of the departed. A columbarium is a structure, room, or space in a mausoleum or other building that is a permanent resting place for cremated remains. It contains niches that are used to hold them.

What fluids do morticians use?

Embalming is a process of chemically preserving tissues with chemical fixatives such as formalin or other fluids that can interfere with toxicological analyses. Common ingredients of embalming fluids are formaldehyde, methanol, sodium borate, sodium nitrate, glycerin, coloring agents, and water.

What group of chemicals is used in funeral preparations in extreme cases, such as bodies with edema or ones exhibiting advanced decomposition?

○ Low index fluids

○ Humectants

○ High index fluids

○ Water conditioning

How do funeral homes keep bodies from smelling?

The most common embalming fluid is a formaldehyde-based solution, which helps to prevent the growth of bacteria and slows down decomposition. Embalming is typically done in funeral homes, and the process usually takes place soon after death.

What fluids are removed during embalming?

Modern embalming now consists primarily of removing all blood and gases from the body and inserting a disinfecting fluid.

What is the best embalming fluid for edema?

Epsom salts has always been advocated in one form or another since the virtual beginning of formaldehyde arterial embalming in the case of edema. Typically a 10% or greater salt solution would be recommended along with a formaldehyde arterial for injection.

What group of chemicals is used in funeral preparations in extreme cases, such as bodies with edema or ones exhibiting advanced decomposition?

  a. Low index fluids

  b. Humectants

  c. High index fluids **Correct**

  d. Water conditioning

High index fluids. High index fluids are for situations in which the preservation demand is high due to the condition of the deceased. These chemicals usually have an index higher than 30. The harsher the conditions of the body, the stronger the primary solution should be. Low index fluids typically have a formaldehyde index in the range of 10 to 18, and it is not advisable to use them in high demand preservation circumstances. The use of these fluids results in the tissue remaining moist and natural with a soft to medium-firm texture. It is not wise to use them in situations where there is high water retention. Humectants are chemicals that increase the tissues' ability to maintain moisture, and aid in preventing dehydration. It would not be advisable to use them in situations where there is already too much moisture, as this would only further inhibit preservation. Water conditioning is an additive agent to remove or render ineffective various chemicals in water that may inhibit drainage or preservation. It does not specifically address the needs that are present in high-demand preservation situations.

Are eyes removed during embalming?

Eyes and lips are not sewn or glued shut. During the embalming process, an "eye cap" is placed under each eyelid and over the eyeball. The eyes themselves may soften a little over time, but the eye cap helps to retain the shape of the eye. A Vaseline-like cream is placed on the lips to keep them together.

How long does it take for embalmed body to smell?

From about day two to four, the microbes are everywhere. And they're producing toxic gases, like ammonia and hydrogen sulfide, which will expand and cause your body to not only bloat, but stink.

When is the correct time to inject tissue builder with a hypodermic syringe?

○ After embalming

○ Before closing the mouth

○ After disinfecting

○ Before embalming

Is the brain removed during embalming?

No. Embalming doesn't remove any organ in the body. Instead, the embalmer replaces the blood with embalming fluid - formaldehyde-based chemicals - through the arteries. For this reason, an embalmed body placed in a casket can last for many years.

What do they do with the blood after embalming?

What happens to the blood and other fluid removed from the body? It is flushed down the drain! Yes, it enters the sewage system and is treated by the wastewater treatment system in whatever town you are in.

How do you reduce swelling after embalming?

Epsom salts can be used to reduce edema in the living and also the dead! Many old school embalmers still use Epsom salts in their arterial solution to battle swelling and edema after death

When is the correct time to inject tissue builder with a hypodermic syringe?

- a. After embalming `Correct`
- b. Before closing the mouth
- c. After disinfecting
- d. Before embalming

After embalming. Tissue builder doesn't contain embalming fluid so it must be used after a corpse has been embalmed to shape treated tissue. If it was used before embalming, the subsequent embalming treatment would not be capable of effectively reaching the tissue that had not been preserved.

Embalming case report

The purpose of an embalming case report is to document the details and procedures of the embalming process for a deceased individual.

> A written record and sketch diagram of the condition of the body upon arrival to the funeral home, the method of embalming, treatments, the times at which the body arrived and preparations were completed, and the license numbers of the embalmers and assistants is called the:
>
> ○ Putrefaction case report
>
> ○ Sanitation case report
>
> ○ Decomposition case report
>
> ○ Embalming case report

What are the 5 steps of the embalming process?

Step 1: Verification of Death. The first step in the embalming process is to verify whether the deceased is in fact dead.

Step 2: Wash and Massage the Body.

Step 3: Setting the Features.

Step 4: Injection of Embalming Fluid.

Step 5: Application of Cosmetics.

How long does a body stay whole after embalming?

After a body is buried and embalmed, preservation of the body may last for a few days to a week. Depending on the humidity, climate, and soil contents, however, the decomposition process may be more rapid. Even the most heavy-duty caskets do not protect against decomposition and the elements.

A written record and sketch diagram of the condition of the body upon arrival to the funeral home, the method of embalming, treatments, the times at which the body arrived and preparations were completed, and the license numbers of the embalmers and assistants is called the:

- a. Putrefaction case report
- b. Sanitation case report
- c. Decomposition case report
- d. Embalming case report **Correct**

The embalming case report. The embalming case report is the all-encompassing written record that includes a drawn sketch diagramming the condition of the body. It identifies the deceased and the embalming practitioner, as well as the chemicals used, the time elapsed, and the funeral home procedures performed. Putrefaction is a term used to describe the decomposition of proteins by diverse enzymes as well as the actions of anaerobic bacteria. It is not the title of a case report. Decomposition is the breakdown of compounds into simpler substances by microbes and autolytic enzymes. The level of decomposition is one finding listed in the embalming case report. Sanitation refers to the documentable efforts to provide for personal and environmental hygiene while working around a corpse. The body and its immediate environment are unsanitary, and create a hazardous condition that could result in an infection to the embalming practitioner. Sanitation is not addressed in a separate report, but the use of chemicals should be listed in the embalming case report so that there is a record of sanitization efforts.

Admittance to the preparation room while a deceased is present should only be granted to:

- ○ Licensees
- ○ Those authorized by the family or the state
- ○ Pre-need counselors
- ○ Both a and b

Admittance to the preparation room while a deceased is present should only be granted to:

a. Licensees

b. Those authorized by the family or the state

c. Pre-need counselors

d. Both a and b **Correct**

Both A: and B: Licensees and those authorized by the family or the state. Any person who has a license to perform work in the preparation room in accordance with the rules and regulations of the state in which they are practicing and the authorization of the business is allowed to be in the prep room. Additionally, any approved family member or state authorized personnel is permitted to be in the prep room. Pre-need counselors typically have no authorization to enter the prep room. They are business agents authorized to represent cemetery and/or funeral products and services to clients in advance of a death.

What is potential pressure in embalming?

Potential pressure. The pressure indicated by the injector gauge needle when the injector motor is running and the arterial tubing is clamped off. Perfusion, circulation of blood within an organ or tissue in adequate amounts to meet current needs of the cells.

The difference between the potential pressure reading and the actual pressure reading indicates the:

○ Vacuum pressure

○ Rate of flow

○ Differential pressure

○ Both b and c

The difference between the potential pressure reading and the actual pressure reading indicates the:

a. Vacuum pressure

b. Rate of flow

c. Differential pressure

d. Both b and c **Correct**

Both b and c, differential pressure and rate of flow. Differential pressure is the difference between the potential pressure reading and the actual pressure reading. It is a gauge of the rate of flow, which is the amount of embalming solution that enters the body in a given period. A vacuum breaker is an accessory device that prevents water from flowing backwards into an unintended water source, which would result in contamination or pollution.

What embalming instrument would be utilized to keep the vein and artery elevated above the incision?

A separator is used to separate vessels from the rest of the body, or raise them above the incision after they have been located. A stopcock can be attached to the embalming tank hose and then to the arterial tube.

A blunt instrument used for tissue dissection and for determining the location and elevation of arteries and veins that is especially useful after the initial incision to locate the carotid artery and jugular vein is made is called.

○ Bistoury knife

○ Hemostat

○ Aneurism needle

○ Forceps

A blunt instrument used for tissue dissection and for determining the location and elevation of arteries and veins that is especially useful after the initial incision to locate the carotid artery and jugular vein is made is called.

   a. Bistoury knife

   b. Hemostat

   c. Aneurism needle **Correct**

   d. Forceps

Aneurism needle. An aneurism needle is a small, razor-sharp medical apparatus used in embalming. It is commonly used to make incisions into tissues, including the initial incision in the corpse for the "raising" of the carotid artery and jugular vein for injection and drainage. A bistoury knife is a long, pointed medical utensil commonly used for removing excess body tissues. A hemostat (forceps) is used to compress blood vessels and limit or prevent blood flow passage or drainage.

The Science of death

Thanatology is the scientific study of death and the losses brought about as a result. It investigates the mechanisms and forensic aspects of death, such as bodily changes that accompany death and the postmortem period, as well as wider psychological and social aspects related to death.

> The study of death and dying that places an emphasis on the psychological and social aspects is called:
>
> ○ Psychology
>
> ○ Psychiatry
>
> ○ Pathology
>
> ○ Thanatology

What does Thanatologist do?

Thanatologists are specialists in a multi-disciplinary field dedicated to better understanding death, dying, grief, loss, and bereavement. They utilize a wide variety of theory and applied practice to support and educate groups and individuals who are navigating end of life issues

What are the stages of death thanatology?

- Primary flaccidity phase or primary relaxation phase.
- Rigor mortis.
- Secondary flaccidity phase or secondary relaxation phase.

The study of death and dying that places an emphasis on the psychological and social aspects is called:

a. Psychology

b. Psychiatry

c. Pathology

d. Thanatology `Correct`

Thanatology. Thanatology is the analysis and study of death and dying and the states of affairs that are pressing on those involved. It evaluates how various factors integrate to influence a person's behavior. Psychology is the analysis and study of human and animal behavior and rationale, including how unique environmental circumstances influence behavior. Psychiatry is the scientific study of both mental and emotional abnormalities in people in order to provide treatment management options. Psychiatry patients include persons affected by a death. Pathology is the scientific examination of diseases in animals, including how the disease was contracted as well as how it affects the physical well-being of the animal.

Agonal hypostasis

It is the settling of blood into the dependent tissues of the body. It occurs as a result of the slowing of circulation just prior to death, which allows the force of gravity to overcome the force of circulation. One of the three circulatory changes during the agonal period.

The process by which blood settles or pools within the vessels to the dependent or lowest parts of the body as a result of gravitational movement is called:

○ Agonal hypostasis

○ Hemolysis

○ Intermittent drainage

○ Agonal mortis

The process by which blood settles or pools within the vessels to the dependent or lowest parts of the body as a result of gravitational movement is called:

a. Agonal hypostasis `Correct`

b. Hemolysis

c. Intermittent drainage

d. Agonal mortis

Agonal hypostasis. Agonal hypostasis is a symptomatic progression by which blood pools and settles in the lowest parts of the body as a result of gravity. Hemolysis occurs when the walls of red blood cells are broken down and the hemoglobin they contain is released. Intermittent drainage (restricted drainage) is a method of drainage used during embalming that stops and starts the drainage at intervals while embalming fluid is being injected. Agonal mortis is the condition that occurs after a person is deceased. There is a progression of temperature reduction as the body temperature of the corpse decreases.

Hydrolysis

Hydrolysis is any chemical reaction in which a molecule of water breaks one or more chemical bonds. The term is used broadly for substitution, elimination, and solvation reactions in which water is the nucleophile.

The chemical reaction in which the chemical bonds of a substance are split by the addition or taking up of water that is also the single most important factor in the initiation of decomposition is called:

○ Hemolysis

○ Hydrolysis

○ Hematemesis

○ Fermentation

The chemical reaction in which the chemical bonds of a substance are split by the addition or taking up of water that is also the single most important factor in the initiation of decomposition is called:

a. Hemolysis

b. Hydrolysis **Correct**

c. Hematemesis

d. Fermentation

Hydrolysis. Hydrolysis in a corpse is a chemical change in which the water in the cadaver splits apart the cells' chemical bonds as the body decomposes. This process is the fundamental accelerator of decomposition. Hemolysis is the process by which red blood cells break down and the hemoglobin they contain is released because it is no longer confined by the cell walls. Hematemesis is the state or condition of a person who is in the act of vomiting blood. Fermentation is a chemical process during which a fluid or solid goes through a chemical change over a period of time and the result is the release of energy.

Rigor mortis can be broken down by which of the following physical methods?

○ Flexing or bending

○ Rotating

○ Massaging the joints

○ All of the above

What are the 3 stages of rigor mortis?

Rigor mortis is one of the most well-known taphonomic alterations, and it is the process by which the body's muscles stiffen, resulting in rigidity, as a result of a variety of chemical changes in the muscle structure.

- Stage I: Autolysis.
- Stage II: Bloat.
- Stage III: Active Decay.

Rigor mortis can be broken down by which of the following physical methods?

a. Flexing or bending

b. Rotating

c. Massaging the joints

d. All of the above `Correct`

All of the above. Rigor mortis can be broken down by the use of physical methods, including flexing, bending, rotating, and massaging the affected joints.

The ventilation of a prep room is measured using the number of air exchanges per hour. This is calculated by taking the total square footage of the room and then determining the size of the air handler or fan needed to move the air out and replace it in a given amount of time. According to Robert Mayer author of Embalming: History, Theory & Practice; the air exchange rate for a preparation room should be between _____ and _____ per hour.

○ 5 – 8

○ 5 – 10

○ 20 – 30

○ 12 – 20

There are approximately six devices that can be used to inject arterial solution. Which of the following is NOT a device historically used during embalming?

○ Bulb syringe

○ Gravity bottle

○ Centrifugal pump

○ Hand pump

The ventilation of a prep room is measured using the number of air exchanges per hour. This is calculated by taking the total square footage of the room and then determining the size of the air handler or fan needed to move the air out and replace it in a given amount of time. According to Robert Mayer author of Embalming: History, Theory & Practice; the air exchange rate for a preparation room should be between _____ and _____ per hour.

a. 5 – 8

b. 5 – 10

c. 20 – 30

d. 12 – 20 **Correct**

12 – 20. Air exchanges per hour refers to the movement of a volume of air in a given period of time. According to the Mortuary College textbook Embalming: History, Theory & Practice by Robert Mayer, the exchange rate should be between 12 and 20 exchanges per hour for ventilation to be considered adequate. Air exchange rates of between 5 – 8 or 5–10 exchanges per hour are not adequate. Air exchange rates of 20 – 30 per hour are higher than necessary.

There are approximately six devices that can be used to inject arterial solution. Which of the following is NOT a device historically used during embalming?

a. Bulb syringe

b. Gravity bottle

c. Centrifugal pump **Correct**

d. Hand pump

Centrifugal pump. The centrifugal pump is a relatively contemporary device compared to all the other choices because it uses an electric pump to produce pressure that can be delivered with or without a pulsating effect. The bulb syringe was a device that was used in the past in embalming. It was manually squeezed to deliver and release pressure and the ensuing flow. The gravity bottle was a frequently used historic technique of embalming that used the force of gravity to move embalming fluids. The hand pump was another device historically used for embalming that relied on the manual action of one's hand to create pressure and move fluid.

Another term used to describe the front, or anterior, of the body is:

○ Dorsal

○ Anatomical position

○ Medial

○ Ventral

A type of suture used to close incisions so that the ligature remains entirely under the epidermis is called:

○ Basket weave suture

○ Intradermal suture

○ Bridge stitch

○ Loop stitch

The natural facial marking that is a small convex distinction found lateral to the end of the line of closure of the mouth is called the:

○ Frontal eminences

○ Angulus oris sulcus

○ Frontal process of the maxilla

○ Angulus oris eminence

Another term used to describe the front, or anterior, of the body is:

a. Dorsal

b. Anatomical position

c. Medial

d. Ventral [Correct]

Ventral. Ventral is an anatomical expression used to refer to the anterior or frontal portion of the human body. Dorsal is an anatomical phrase used to describe the posterior or rear of the human body. Anatomical position is the recognized scientific standard of how a human body should be situated so that all directions and positions are determined in the same way. Medial refers to the midline area (medial plane) of the human body.

A type of suture used to close incisions so that the ligature remains entirely under the epidermis is called:

a. Basket weave suture

b. Intradermal suture [Correct]

c. Bridge stitch

d. Loop stitch

Intradermal suture. The intradermal suture (hidden suture) is used to secure incisions so the ligature remains concealed under the skin. The basket weave suture (cross stitch) is a system of stitches that crosses the limits of an excision to secure fillers and hold tissues in their proper positions. The bridge stitch (interrupted suture) is a short-term suture made up of divided pieces that are tied to hold the tissue in its proper position. They are removed later. The loop stitch is a single stitch used to secure restorative materials.

To ensure a successful application, an embalmer will usually apply surface mortuary wax to a deceased:

○ Approximately three to six hours after embalming

○ Immediately after embalming is completed

○ Before embalming is started

○ Not less than twenty-four hours after embalming

The natural facial marking that is a small convex distinction found lateral to the end of the line of closure of the mouth is called the:

a. Frontal eminences

b. Angulus oris sulcus

c. Frontal process of the maxilla

d. Angulus oris eminence **Correct**

Angulus oris eminence. The angulus oris eminence is a natural face marking that consists of a comparatively undersized, convex, raised area found lateral to the end of the line of closure of the mouth. The angulus oris sulcus is a natural facial marking groove found at each end of the line of closure of the mouth. The frontal process of the maxilla is the raised part of the upper jaw that protrudes slightly as it rises alongside the nasal bone to meet the frontal bone in the upper jaw. The frontal eminences are a pair of distinctive raised areas of the frontal bone found roughly one inch beneath the normal hairline.

To ensure a successful application, an embalmer will usually apply surface mortuary wax to a deceased:

a. Approximately three to six hours after embalming **Correct**

b. Immediately after embalming is completed

c. Before embalming is started

d. Not less than twenty-four hours after embalming

Approximately three to six hours after embalming. Most funeral homes will allow several hours to pass after embalming before applying mortuary wax so the tissue is treated and becomes firm and dry. Restorative wax is typically applied to replace skin and make a "skin-like surface" from an area of fever blisters, abrasions, or burns. Surface wax needs to be applied to embalmed tissue. At least three hours of setting time is required following embalming for the embalming treatment to infiltrate and dry all tissues. The application of surface wax to tissue immediately after embalming is not recommended since the surface areas of the deceased at this point are not preserved or firm. It is not necessary to wait 24 hours for the tissues to reach a sufficient state of preservation before applying mortuary wax.

The most common of the basic linear forms of facial profiles is called:

○ Vertical balanced profile

○ Convex profile

○ Concave profile

○ Horizontally balanced profile

The most common of the basic linear forms of facial profiles is called:

a. Vertical balanced profile

b. Convex profile [Correct]

c. Concave profile

d. Horizontally balanced profile

Convex profile. The convex profile is the most common profile form among human beings. In this form, a person's forehead posteriorly recedes from the eyebrows and the chin recedes from the upper lip. A vertically balanced profile is when the chin, forehead, and upper lip are all situated in a related alignment so none of them protrude or recede more than the other two features. A concave profile is when the forehead of the person protrudes further than the eyebrows and the chin protrudes beyond the plane of the upper lip. There is no such thing as a horizontal balanced profile.

A suture made around a circular opening or puncture that closes the margins when it is pulled is called a:

○ Basket weave suture

○ Purse suture

○ Bridge suture

○ Whip suture

A type of incomplete fracture in which the bone may become bent or broken but does not go through the skin is called a:

○ Compound fracture

○ Third degree fracture

○ Open fracture

○ Closed or greenstick fracture

A suture made around a circular opening or puncture that closes the margins when it is pulled is called a:

- a. Basket weave suture
- b. Purse suture **Correct**
- c. Bridge suture
- d. Whip suture

Purse suture. A purse suture is a stitch that is used to close a rounded opening. It is made by stitching around the perimeter and pulling the stitches firmly to close the borders of the opening. The basket weave suture (cross stitch) is a system of stitches that traverses the boundaries of an incision and is used to secure fillers and keep body tissues in place. The bridge suture (interrupted suture) is a transitory suture consisting of independently cut and tied stitches that is used to maintain the location of tissues. The whip suture is used to secure elongated incisions, such as those made during an autopsy.

A type of incomplete fracture in which the bone may become bent or broken but does not go through the skin is called a:

- a. Compound fracture
- b. Third degree fracture
- c. Open fracture
- d. Closed or greenstick fracture **Correct**

Closed or greenstick fracture. A greenstick fracture is a bowed or unfinished fracture (closed fracture) because the broken bone does not perforate the skin and there is no exposed bone. A compound fracture is a type of fracture in which the wound causes the broken bone to slice and push through the skin. Third degree is not a fracture classification, but is used to classify burns when the victim's skin tissues have been charred. An open fracture is the same as a compound fracture. In this type of fracture, an injury causes a broken bone to pierce through the skin.

The Funeral Director

The funeral director is responsible for filing an accurate and complete death certificate with the proper registration official, although state laws vary in specific requirements. The death certificate is a permanent legal record of the fact of death of a person. As a permanent legal record, the certificate is extremely important to the decedent's family. It is also needed for a variety of medical and health-related research efforts.

The death certificate provides important information about the decedent (e.g., age, sex, race and ethnicity, education, date of death, names of parents, and, if married, name of spouse), the circumstances and cause of death, and final disposition. This information is used in the application for insurance benefits, settlement of pension claims, and transfer of title of real and personal property. The certificate is considered prima facie evidence of the fact of death and can be introduced in court as evidence when a question about the death arises. An accurate death record is the responsibility of the funeral director, both as a service to the decedent's family and as the cornerstone of the nation's death registration system.

In general, funeral directors' duties are to:

- Complete, or have completed, all items on the death certificate.
- Obtain the cause-of-death information and certification statement from the attending physician or the medical examiner or coroner.

- Secure the signature of the person pronouncing death on the certificate, and review the certificate for completeness and accuracy.
- File the certificate with the proper state or local official within the time limit specified by the vital statistics laws of the state.
- Notify the medical examiner or coroner of any death that is believed to have been due to an accident, suicide, or homicide, or to have occurred without medical attendance, unless the pronouncing or certifying physician or the police have already done so.
- Obtain and use all necessary permits and other forms associated with the death registration system.
- Cooperate with state or local registrars concerning queries on certificate entries.
- Cooperate with pathologists in cases involving postmortem examinations.
- Be thoroughly familiar with all laws, rules, and regulations governing the vital statistics system.
- Call on the local or state office of vital statistics for advice and assistance when necessary.
- Where the place of death is unknown, complete and file the certificate of death in accordance with the laws of the state in which the body was found.

The Centers for Disease Control concluded that funeral directors had an elevated risk of contracting a variety of bloodborne and airborne pathogens as a result of their contact with dead human bodies, and found that the most frequently reported diseases by funeral directors included:

○ Hematoma

○ Staphylococcal infection

○ Cutaneous tuberculosis

○ Both b and c

The Centers for Disease Control concluded that funeral directors had an elevated risk of contracting a variety of bloodborne and airborne pathogens as a result of their contact with dead human bodies, and found that the most frequently reported diseases by funeral directors included:

a. Hematoma

b. Staphylococcal infection

c. Cutaneous tuberculosis

d. Both b and c **Correct**

Both B: and C: The Centers for Disease Control (CDC) has determined through studies conducted with practicing funeral directors that the most common bloodborne and airborne pathogens contracted through exposure to dead human bodies are staphylococcal infections and cutaneous (skin) tuberculosis. A staphylococcal infection is a very contagious malady that can be transmitted from person to person from droplets from the nose of an infected person or from the bacteria in the pus oozing out of an infected lesion. Cutaneous tuberculosis (TB) is tuberculosis on the skin caused by the mycobacterium tuberculosis, and if the embalmer is exposed to this a skin infection called tuberculosis chancre may occur. A hematoma is due to a leaking blood vessel, and results in an area with a collected pool of blood.

Test Questions

1. A funeral rite that is adjusted to the needs and wants of those involved is known as

A. adaptive.

B. humanistic.

C. traditional.

D. a memorial service.

2. In the late 19th century, funeral services were usually held in the

A. home.

B. funeral home.

C. city hall.

D. church building.

3. The third stage of anticipatory grief described by Kubler-Ross is

A. anger.

B. bargaining.

C. denial.

D. depression.

The most common of the basic linear forms of facial profiles is called:

○ Vertical balanced profile

○ Convex profile

○ Concave profile

○ Horizontally balanced profile

4. What type of damages pay over and above the actual loss?

A. token

B. nominal

C. punitive

D. compensatory

5. Clothes and jewelry given to the funeral director to be placed on the decedent's body are considered in law as

A. no property.

B. quasi-property.

C. bailed property.

D. unclaimed property.

6. The proper title for an officiant of the Christian Science faith is a

A. pastor.

B. priest.

C. reader.

D. speaker.

7. Which of the following in NOT specifically required by the Federal Trade Commission (FTC)?

A. Casket Price List

B. Outer Burial Container Price List

C. Funeral Agreement Form

D. General Price List

8. Traditionally, the name given to a symbolic cloth covering placed over the casket is a(n)

A. pall.

B. veil.

C. cape.

D. interment cover.

9. In casket manufacturing, kapok is used as a

A. lining material.

B. padding material.

C. casket covering material.

D. backing material.

10. Gross sales minus sales returns and allowances, and minus discounts on sales yields, are

A. total purchases.

B. operating expenses.

C. gross profit.

D. net sales.

Key

1. A
2. A
3. B
4. C
5. C
6. C
7. C
8. A
9. B
10. D

SCIENCES SAMPLE QUESTIONS

1. A factor that indicates the use of a MORE dilute arterial solution is

A. thick skin.

B. tough skin.

C. emaciation.

D. hydration.

2. Rigor mortis and algor mortis are similar in that both are

A. before death.

B. forms of edema.

C. stiffened conditions.

D. postmortem conditions.

3. The direction of eyebrow hair growth is laterally

A. upward.

B. upward and inward.

C. upward and outward.

D. downward and outward.

4. Hypodermic tissue building may be performed as a post embalming treatment for

A. emaciation.

B. tissue swelling.

C. controlling purge.

D. body fluid accumulation.

5. Pathogenic microbes are most virulent

A. after the first 24 hours.

B. during thermal death time.

C. only in the presence of dry heat.

D. when first emitted from the body.

6. Inflammation of the sac surrounding the heart is called

A. myocarditis.

B. pancreatitis.

C. endocarditis.

D. pericarditis.

7. Chemicals that have the capability of displacing unpleasant odors are

A. humectants.

B. deodorants.

C. surfactants.

D. disinfectants.

8. Which of the following is characteristic of a jaundice fluid?

A. no bleach content

B. no counter staining

C. low formaldehyde content

D. high formaldehyde content

9. The external iliac artery lies along the medial border of which of the following muscles?

A. psoas major

B. coracobrachialis

C. pectoralis major

D. external oblique

10. When using the 9-region method for cavity embalming, the cecum is located in which of the following regions?

A. hypogastric

B. right lumbar

C. left inguinal

D. right inguinal

Key

1. C
2. D
3. C
4. A
5. D
6. D
7. B
8. C
9. A
10. D

Embalming: Test Questions

1. A process of chemically treating the dead human body to reduce the presence and growth of microorganisms, to retard organic decomposition, and to restore an acceptable physical appearance is: Embalming

2. The irreversible cessation of all vital functions is: Death

3. Those changes occurring in the interval prior to somatic death are: Antemortem

4. A sharp cutting instrument used for making incisions is the: Scalpel

5. That consideration given to the dead body, prior to, during and after the embalming procedure is complete is: Case analysis

6. An imaginary line drawn on the surface of the skin to represent the approximate location of some deeper underlying structure is the: Linear guide

7. Injection and drainage from one location is called: One point injection

8. Chemicals which inactivate saprophytic bacteria are called: Preservative

9. The movement of embalming solutions from the point of injection throughout the arterial system and into the capillaries is called: Distribution

10. This embalming method consists of injecting a few ounces of arterial chemical, stopping injection, then draining for a few minutes, and then repeating the process: Alternate

11. This is a term used to refer to the after-death examination of the organs and tissues of a body to determine cause of death or pathological conditions: Postmortem

12. Any abnormal color appearing in or upon the human body is called: Discoloration

13. A needle injector is used for this purpose: Mouth closure

14. What is often aspirated from the stomach: Hydrochloric acid

15. When death has been due to pneumonia, an embalmer should expect: Thoracic congestion and increased blood viscosity

16. The Formaldehyde Standard for short-term exposure to formaldehyde is: 2 ppm/15 minutes

17. Signs of death exhibited by the eyes of the deceased include: Clouding of the cornea and flattening of the eyeball, Loss of luster of the conjunctiva, Pupil dilation and non-response to light

18. Another name for pleural effusion is: Hydrothorax

19. Proteolysis refers to decomposition of: Proteins

20. Which conditions would require special attention during thoracic cavity embalming? Hydrothorax

21. Discoloration resulting when formaldehyde reacts with hemoglobin in the tissues is called: Formaldehyde grey

22. Severe generalized edema is known as: Anasarca

23. Escape of blood serum from an intravascular to an extravascular location immediately before death is: Agonal edema

24. Low index fluids used to inhibit bilirubin from turning to biliverdin are known as: Jaundice fluids

25. Chemicals that create an increased capability for embalmed tissues to retain their moisture are called: Humectants

26. How many ounces of formaldehyde are contained in a 16-ounce bottle of 25 index arterial fluid? 4 ounces

www.ingramcontent.com/pod-product-compliance
Lightning Source LLC
Chambersburg PA
CBHW071904070526
44583CB00016B/1830